TRUE story Bible

14 true stories about JESUS

by Akram Zaki

Illustrated by Paulo Gaviola

First Printing: January 2025

Please consider requesting that a copy of this volume be purchased by your local library system.

ISBN: 978-1-68344-410-7
ISBN: 978-1-61458-925-9 (digital)
Printed in China

Please visit our website for other great titles:
www.masterbooks.com

For information regarding promotional opportunities, please contact the publicity department at pr@nlpg.com.

Master Books®
A Division of New Leaf Publishing Group
www.masterbooks.com

Table of Contents

The *True Story Bible* is a children's Bible designed to make understanding God's love and redemption accessible and meaningful to young hearts. Each story within the series draws from beloved Bible accounts, explaining Jesus' atoning work on the Cross in language that children can grasp.

Each narrative opens with the story's place in Scripture, clearly showing that these accounts are rooted in the Bible, not fictionalized stories. This approach helps children see the reliability of Scripture and understand that God's Word is true and alive today. With stories drawn from both the Old and New Testaments, each reading demonstrates God's unwavering faithfulness, His promises, and His love and care for us.

Whether reading this together as a family or using it in children's ministry, the *True Story Bible* encourages young readers to build a foundation of faith early on. Every story reinforces that God's promises are trustworthy, emphasizing key lessons about His love and His desire for us to know Him.

True Stories from the Old Testament

ADAM and EVE

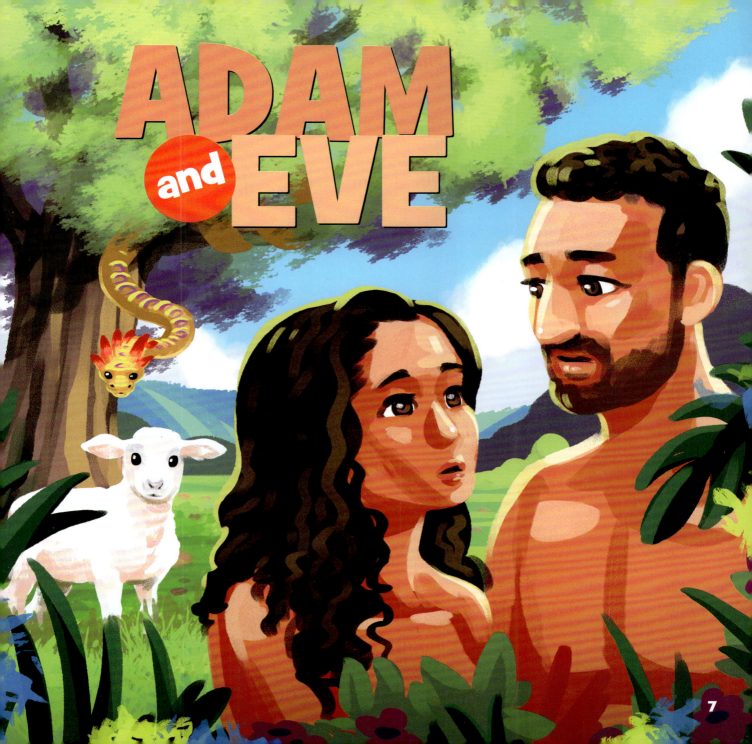

This is a true story.

It comes from
Genesis Chapter 2 and 3
in your Bible.

This story has some hidden things to look out for.

See if you can find them:

In the beginning,
God created EVERYTHING.

Big things,
tiny things,
all living kinds,
stars and planets, too!

11

Then God made a human.

A man called Adam.

People were special to God.

He placed Adam in a special garden and gave him the responsibility of naming all the animals.

Out of Adam's rib, God made Eve.
They would be a family
to watch over the Earth,
and fill it with new humans.

They would take care of the animals,
and grow the garden
until it filled the Earth.

God loved Adam and Eve and He spoke to them.

He gave them good things and was kind to them. He gave them the Tree of Life, so they could live forever.

He even gave them a way to show their love for Him, by obeying Him.

"You can eat of the fruit of any tree in the garden," God said.

"Except for the tree of the Knowledge of Good and Evil. For if you eat of that tree, you will die."

Life was good for Adam and Eve,
until one day, a serpent came
and spoke to her.

He tricked Eve into eating the fruit
God had told them not to eat.

Adam also ate the fruit.
But Adam wasn't tricked into it.

He chose to disobey.

16

All of a sudden, Adam and Eve felt things they had never felt before: shame, guilt, and fear.

For the first time they were ashamed that they had no clothes on. So they tried making clothes for themselves out of fig leaves.

Then they heard God coming.

They ran and hid, afraid of Him for the first time.

God found them
(of course He did).

"Have you eaten the fruit I told you not to?" He asked.

They should have said "Sorry," then and there, but they didn't.

Eve blamed the serpent.

Adam blamed Eve.

Adam even tried to blame God.

19

Just as God had promised,
Adam and Eve's sin
led to death.

But it wasn't Adam and Eve
that died that day.

God killed an animal.

He took its skin and made clothes out of it to cover Adam and Eve from their shame because they were uncovered.

God made them a promise:
one day He would send a Savior
to cover the sin, shame, and
guilt of the world, just like
He had covered them.

God didn't want people to
eat from the Tree of Life
and live forever,
stuck in their sin.

That would be worse
than death.

So, Adam and Eve had to leave the garden forever.

But God never left them.

He never stopped loving them either. And God never forgot about the promise He made to them.

Did you find the hidden pictures?

They can help to summarize our story.

God's perfect rules

Sinful choices

A failed attempt to cover up

God provides a covering

25

What do you think?

Is this a story that tells us never to eat fruit?

NO.

Is this a story that tells us to make clothes out of leaves?

NO.

So what's this story really about?

This story is about JESUS!

But how?

The Bible says that just like Adam and Eve, we have ALL chosen to disobey God and what He tells us to do.

This is the reason why death and sadness exists in our world.

But just like God still loved Adam and Eve,

He very much still loves us too.

27

Adam and Eve deserved to die that day, but God was merciful.

He was kind, and generous, and loving, just like He always is.

God killed an animal to provide a covering for Adam and Eve so they wouldn't be ashamed.

God sent His Son, Jesus, to die on the Cross.

Jesus covers us from our sin, shame, and guilt when we believe in Him.

Adam and Eve tried to cover themselves their own way, but God gave them a better covering. Adam and Eve had to choose to take it or reject it.

Sometimes we think we can cover our sin and guilt our own way.

God gave us a better covering for our sin too.

We need to accept Jesus as Savior or reject Him.

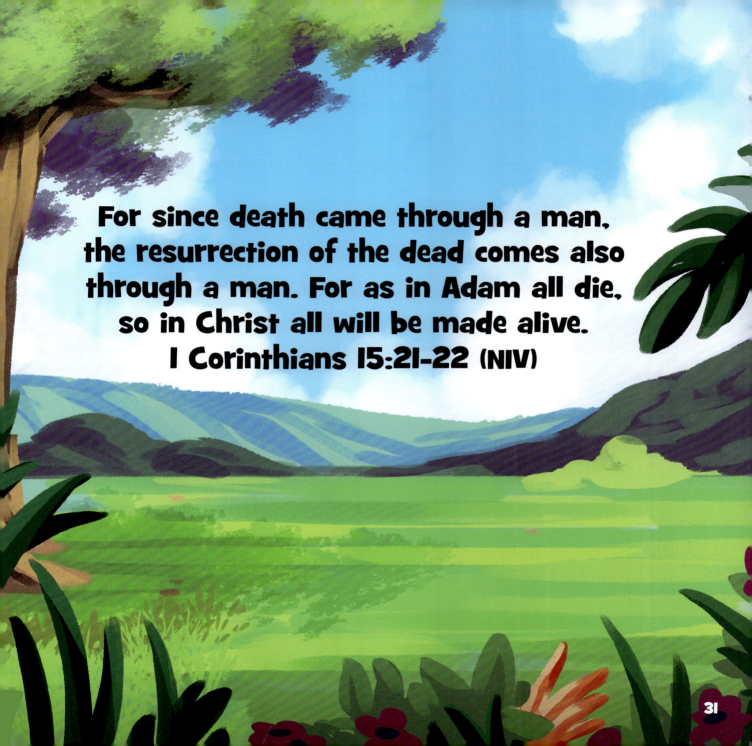

For since death came through a man, the resurrection of the dead comes also through a man. For as in Adam all die, so in Christ all will be made alive.
I Corinthians 15:21-22 (NIV)

So next time you hear the wonderful, true story about Adam and Eve, remember... it's a story that tells us about Jesus!

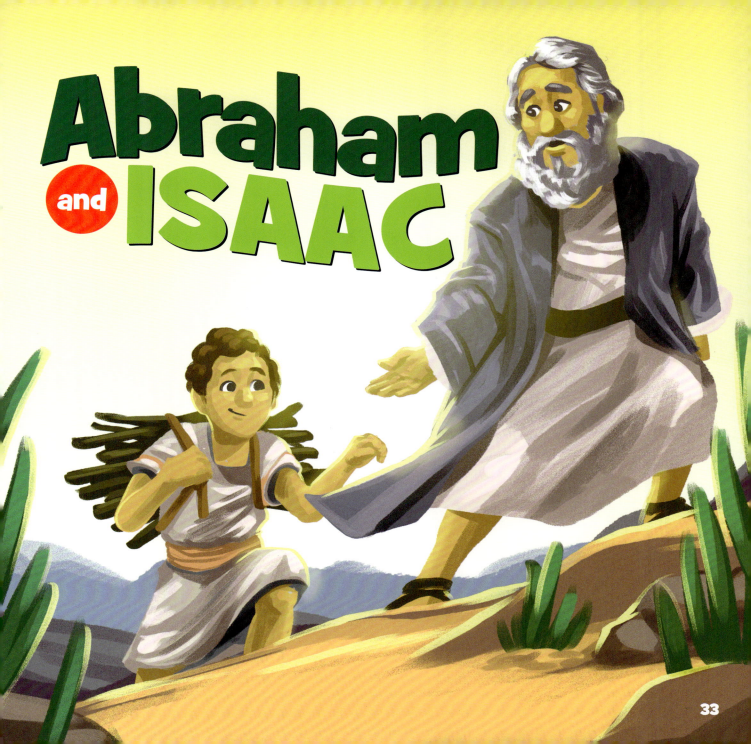

Abraham and ISAAC

This is a true story.

It comes from Genesis
Chapter 22 in your Bible.

This story has some hidden things to look out for.

See if you can find them:

Long ago in Bible times, people used to make sacrifices to God. God had taught them that disobeying Him (sin) deserved death. But God loved them and gave them a way out. Instead of them dying, God told them to sacrifice a lamb.

When people saw that the lamb had died, it reminded them that God was serious about sin but that He had provided a way for them to escape, because in a way, the lamb had died in their place.

This story happened back then.

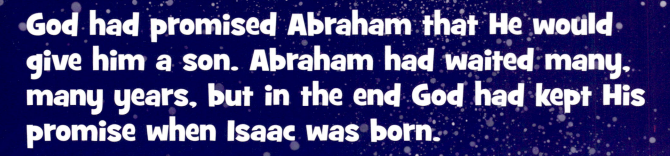

God had promised Abraham that He would give him a son. Abraham had waited many, many years, but in the end God had kept His promise when Isaac was born.

Abraham loved his son.
He loved him more than
anything else in this world.

One night God spoke to Abraham.

"Abraham. Take your son, your beloved son, to a high mountain I will show you. On that mountain, I want you to sacrifice him to me as a burnt offering."

Abraham loved Isaac. But Abraham knew that God was good, that He knew what He was doing, and that He needed to be obeyed.

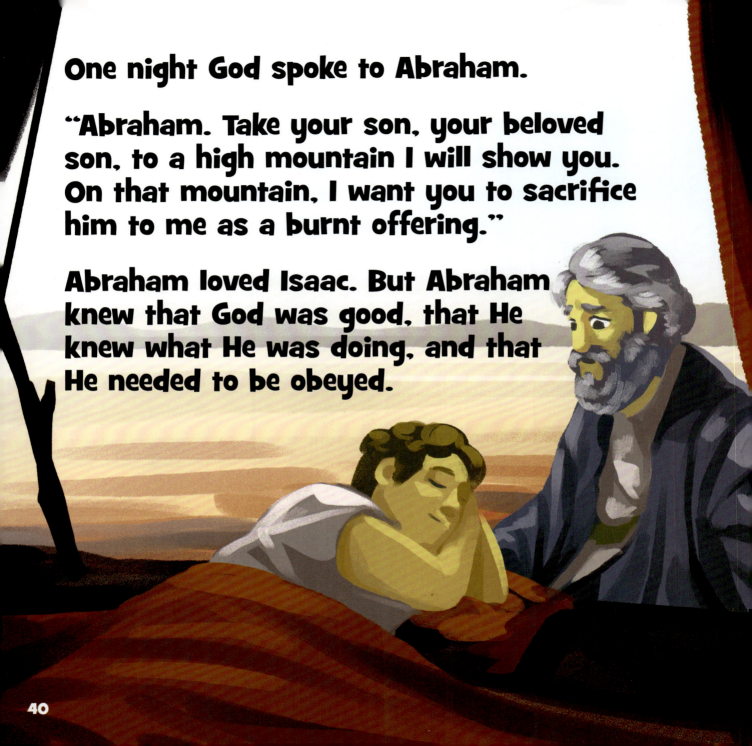

The next morning, Abraham took a donkey, loaded it up with wood for the sacrifice, flints to make fire, and then took his son Isaac with him.

"We have the wood and the fire for the offering," said Isaac, "But where is the lamb for the sacrifice?"

"God will provide the lamb, my son," Abraham replied.

Abraham and Isaac walked for three days until they got to a high mountain.

They left the donkey at the bottom of the mountain, and Isaac carried the wood up the mountain.

There they built an altar out of rocks and put the wood on top of it.

Abraham placed Isaac on the altar.

Abraham took out his knife, but the angel of God called to him.

"Abraham, stop! Do not lay a hand on your son. Now I know that you fear me. For you have not held back your beloved son from me."

Abraham looked up, and in a bush nearby was a ram (a male sheep) caught by its horns. He went over and took the ram and sacrificed it as a burnt offering instead of his son.

God accepted the sacrifice and forgave Abraham and his family for their sins. God was pleased with Abraham because he had trusted Him.

Did you find the hidden pictures?
They can help to summarize our story.

A beloved son

A high mountain

**A sacrifice that
God provides**

Is this a story that teaches us to avoid going mountain climbing with our dads?
NO.

Is this a story that tells us that sheep get stuck in bushes a lot?
NO.

So what's this story really about?

This story is about JESUS!

But how?

The Bible tells us that sacrificing lambs and sheep could never really pay for the wrong things we have done, but those lambs are just a reminder of God's promise to rescue us from sin.

The Bible says that God has a beloved son, Jesus.

Jesus came to Earth, was born as a human, and grew up into a man.

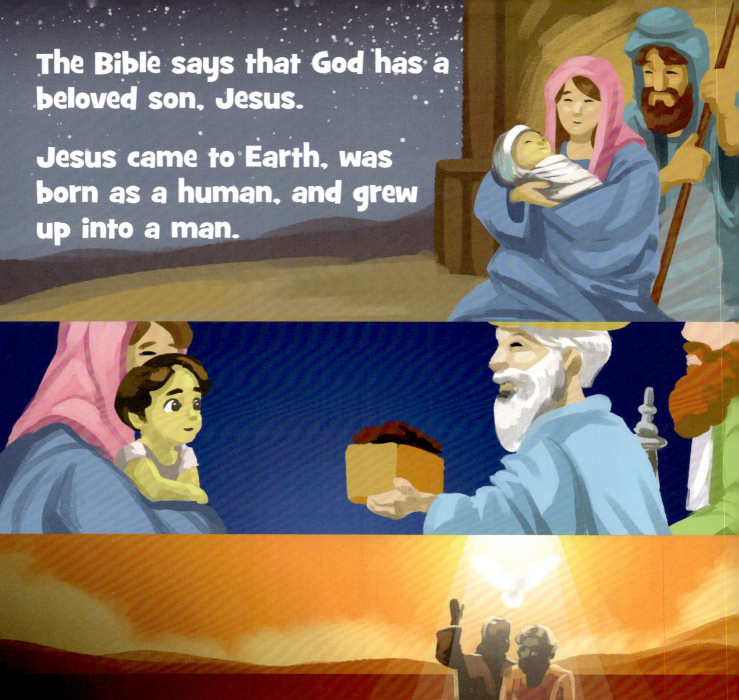

Jesus lived a perfect life, always doing what was right, and never what was wrong.

Jesus, God's beloved Son, climbed a high mountain. It was called Calvary. He did it carrying wood on His back too, a wooden cross.

God knew that we could never pay for our own sin, so He provided the sacrifice needed.

Jesus was the sacrifice that God provided.

Jesus dying on the Cross shows us how serious God is about sin, but also, how much He loves us. God has provided a way for us to be rescued because Jesus has died in our place.

53

Jesus came back from the dead, proving that He had paid for our sin, and because of this, we can trust Him to rescue us!

For God so loved the world that he gave his one and only Son, that whoever believes in him shall not perish but have eternal life.
John 3:16 (NIV)

The next time you hear the wonderful true story about Abraham and Isaac, remember... it's a story that tells us about Jesus!

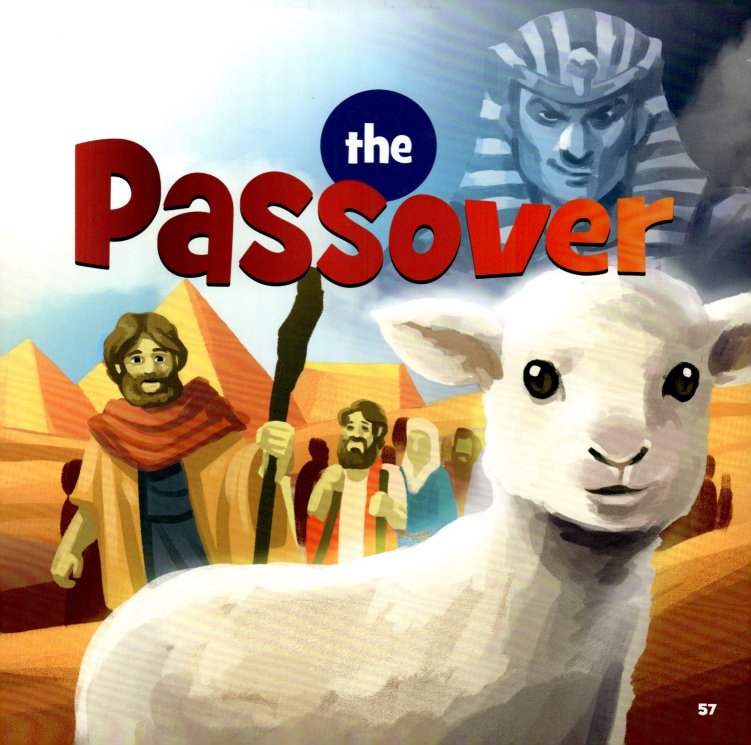

the Passover

This is a true story.

It comes from Exodus
Chapter 12 in your Bible.

This story has some hidden things to look out for.

See if you can find them:

God's chosen people, the Israelites, were slaves in Egypt. The Pharaoh was a bad man who made their lives difficult and miserable.

He refused to let them go, even when God sent Moses to tell him that he must.

God sent many amazing signs to warn the Pharaoh and the Egyptians to let His people go, like plagues of frogs and flies, but the Pharaoh refused to listen.

So, God told Moses there would be one more sign. God would bring judgment on the land of Egypt. God said that after this, the Pharaoh would have no choice but to let His people go so they could live in freedom and worship Him.

Judgment was going to come on the whole land, on everyone, Israelites and Egyptians. If anyone wanted to escape this judgment, that family would have to kill a lamb, and put its blood on the doorposts of their house.

Then they would roast the lamb and eat it together with their family.

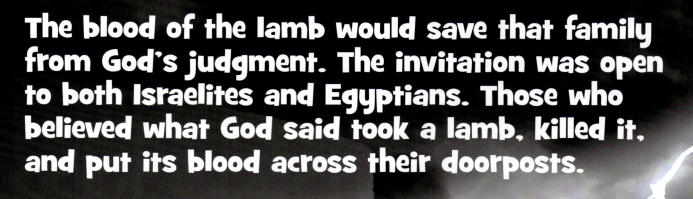

The blood of the lamb would save that family from God's judgment. The invitation was open to both Israelites and Egyptians. Those who believed what God said took a lamb, killed it, and put its blood across their doorposts.

On the night of the Passover, God passed through the land, and His judgment fell on everyone who did not obey what God had said.

Whenever God saw the blood of the lamb on a doorpost, He passed over that house, just like He promised.

In the morning, the Pharaoh was defeated.
God's judgment had come down on him
and his family, and everyone else who
had not obeyed God's command.

The Pharaoh let the Israelites go.

They were free to live, and free to worship God.

All because of a lamb.

God told the Israelites to remember what He had done for them, and to celebrate it each year with a special holiday. That holiday is called Passover, because God passed over them, and rescued them from slavery.

Did you find the hidden pictures?
They can help to summarize our story.

Helpless slaves

Coming judgment

A slain lamb

Freedom

Is this a story that teaches us to have barbecues with our family?
NO.

Is this a story that tells us why some people don't like frogs?
NO.

So what's this story really about?

This story is about JESUS!

But how?

The Bible says that we are slaves, not to an evil Pharaoh, but to sin and death. We all think, say, and do things that disappoint God. So God is sending judgment. Not because He hates us, but because it is the right thing to do.

The problem is that if God judges us, we will all be in trouble.

So, just like the story of the Passover,
God makes a way for us to be saved.

There was a prophet called John the Baptist, who saw Jesus one day. John pointed to Jesus and said something strange. He said "Look! The LAMB of God who takes away the sin of the world."

John the Baptist was remembering the lamb that was killed, so that those who believed God would be safe.

Just like that lamb at Passover was killed and its blood poured out, Jesus was also killed and His blood was poured out. In fact, Jesus died on the anniversary of Passover. This is because Passover was really all about Jesus.

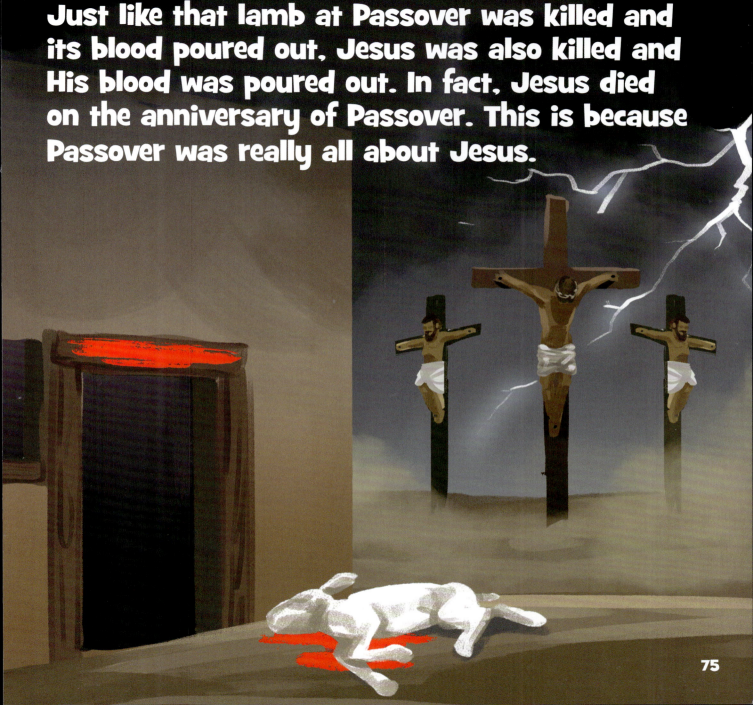

The Passover story is about how God saves us by the death of His son Jesus, the true Lamb of God.

Because of Jesus, God's judgment has passed over us too, and we can be free from our sin and death.

We can be free from our
sin and death when we
receive His salvation!

The next day John saw Jesus coming toward him and said, "Look, the Lamb of God, who takes away the sin of the world!"

John 1:29 (NIV)

So next time you hear the wonderful, true story about the Passover, remember... it's really a story about Jesus!

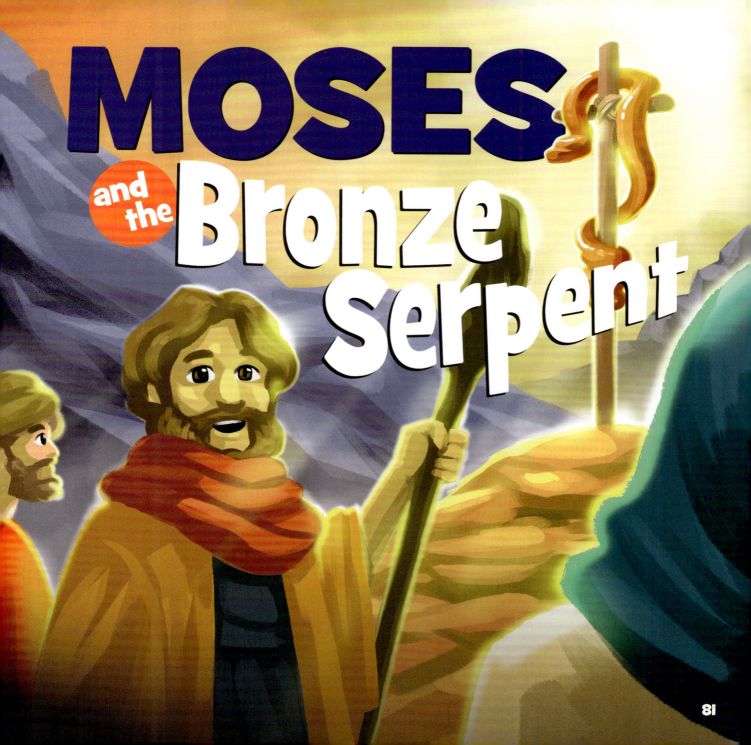

MOSES and the Bronze Serpent

This is a true story.

82

It comes from Numbers Chapter 21 in your Bible.

This story has some hidden things to look out for.

See if you can find them:

God's chosen people, the Israelites, were living in the wilderness.

God took care of their needs. He gave them water and food and kept them safe from their enemies. He made their clothes and shoes never wear out and even guided them with a huge pillar of fire and cloud. But the Israelites complained and complained and complained.

They were rude and disobedient. They were ungrateful for all God had given them, didn't give God the respect He deserved, and didn't trust Him.

They had also done many evil things and needed to be taught the right way to live.

So God sent venomous snakes.

The snakes bit the Israelites, killing many people and making many more horribly sick.

The Israelites realized that what they had done was wrong and asked God to forgive them.

Even though God had sent a punishment, this didn't mean He didn't love them. God would always love them, even when they were wrong.

God told Moses to do something strange.

"Make a bronze snake and put it on a pole. If anyone is bitten by a snake, that person should look at the bronze snake on the pole. Then that person will get better."

So Moses made a bronze snake and put it up on a pole.

It seemed strange that the way to recover from a venomous snake bite would be to look at a snake on a pole, but God was actually calling His people to trust and obey Him.

The people who trusted God's words and looked at the snake were healed, and they lived.

But those who didn't died.

God continued to take care of His people in the wilderness, and in time, led them to their new home.

Did you find the hidden things?
They can help summarize our story.

People disobey

Bad news

God provides a way

People have to choose

Is this a story that teaches us
the secrets of medicine?

NO.

Is this a story that teaches us to be extra
careful of snakes when we are hiking?

NO.
(Even though that IS a good idea!)

So then what's this story really about?

This story is about JESUS!

But how?

In another part of the Bible, called the Book of John, chapter 3, Jesus was having a conversation with a man called Nicodemus.

Jesus told Nicodemus that the story of the bronze snake was really about Him.

But how?

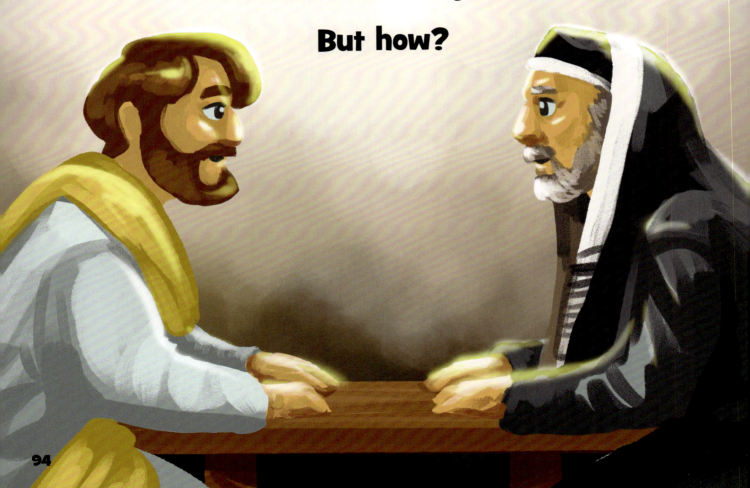

The Bible says that we are just like the Israelites. God takes care of us, but we don't always obey Him. We are often disrespectful, ungrateful, and rude.

The Bible calls this SIN.

Every one of us has sinned before.

It also says that the punishment of sin is death.

BAD NEWS.

But the Bible also tells us that God loves us and provides a way for us to be saved.

God sent His son Jesus to rescue us.

God had told the Israelites that if they trusted and obeyed Him by looking at the bronze snake, then they would be saved.

Just like the bronze snake was hung up for the Israelites to see, Jesus was also hung up on a wooden cross, for everyone to see.

God tells us to do the same. To trust and obey God by looking to Jesus and trusting He can save us.

And He will.

Jesus said,

"Just as Moses lifted up the snake in the wilderness, so the Son of Man must be lifted up, that everyone who believes may have eternal life in him." For God so loved the world that he gave his one and only Son, that whoever believes in him shall not perish but have eternal life.

John 3:14-16 (NIV)

So next time you hear the wonderful true story about the bronze serpent, remember...

It's a story that tells us about Jesus!

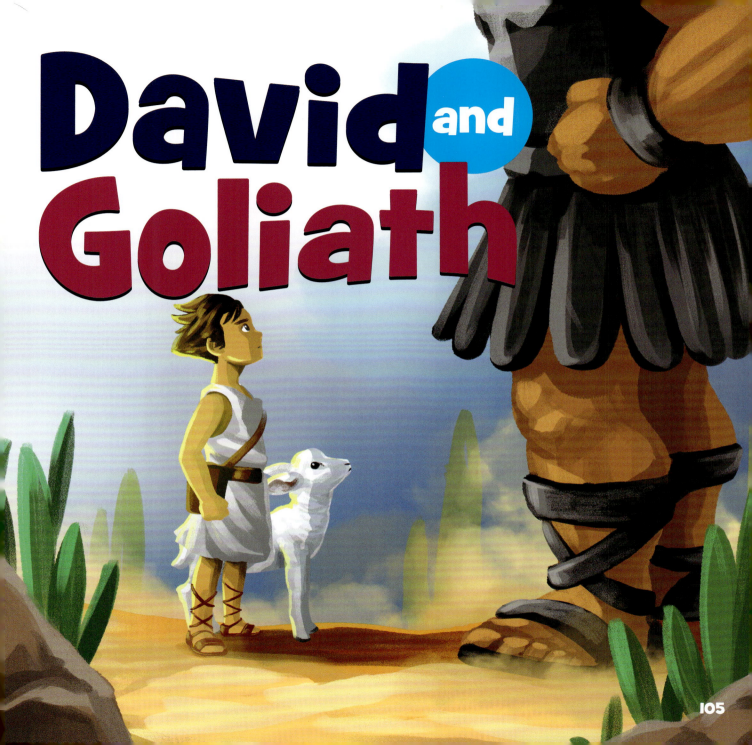

David and Goliath

This is a true story.

It comes from I Samuel Chapter 17 in your Bible.

This story has some hidden things to look out for.

See if you can find them:

In the Bible, God's chosen people, the Israelites, had many enemies. One group was called the Philistines.

The Philistines made war with the Israelites, A LOT.

One day, the Philistines called up a champion. His name was Goliath.

Goliath was a giant. **ACTUALLY, A GIANT.** He was strong and tough and a man of war. He had a spear, a sword, and a shield.

Goliath challenged the Israelites. He stood in the valley between the armies and yelled, "Choose for yourselves a champion and let him fight me. If he wins, we will surrender to you, but if he loses, then you must surrender to us."

The Israelites were afraid, and they couldn't choose a champion because no one in their army was strong enough to defeat Goliath.

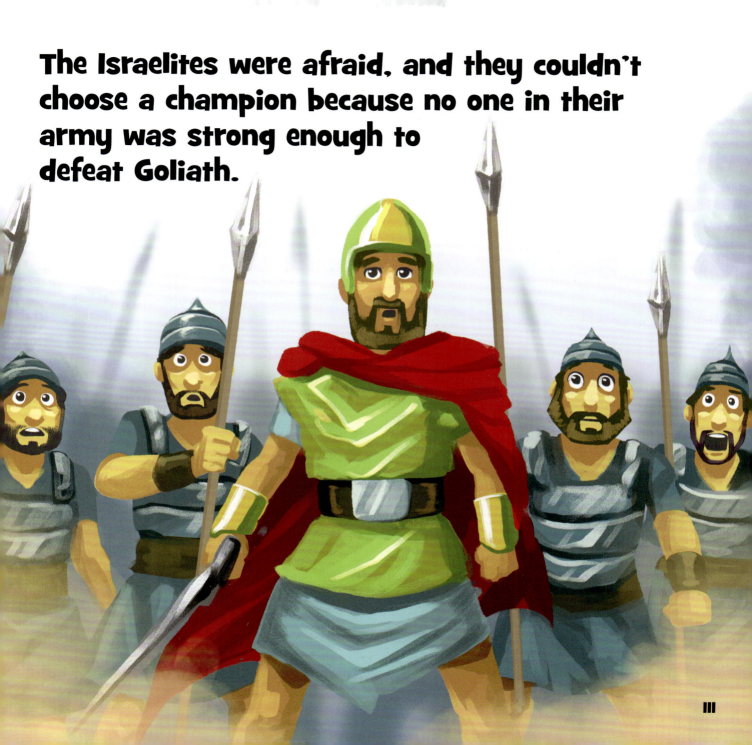

III

A young shepherd boy named David came to the Israelite army to visit his brothers and deliver some food from their father.

David heard Goliath's challenge and saw everyone's fear.

David wasn't afraid.

"I'll do it," he said.

"God will help me. He is bigger than this puny giant."

David refused to use armor and weapons that the army had.

He had his own way.

David collected five smooth stones from a riverbed. He put one in his slingshot and spun it round and round, faster and faster.

"Hey, you!" David said to the giant.

"You may have a sword and spear, but I am on God's side, and He is much bigger than you!"

David flung the stone, it flew through the air, and smashed straight into Goliath's head.

The giant crashed to the ground.

The battle was over.

The Israelite army didn't need to be afraid anymore.

God had used David to save the day.

Some years after this story,
David, the hero, became king.

Did you find the hidden pictures?

They can help to summarize our story.

An unstoppable enemy

An unexpected hero

An incredible victory

God's chosen king

What do you think?

Is this a story that teaches
us to fight big people?
NO.

Is this a story that tells us that
slingshots are better than swords?
NO.

So, what's this story really about?

This story is about JESUS!

But how?

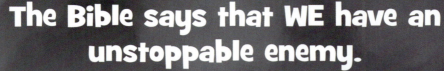

The Bible says that WE have an unstoppable enemy.

Death.

Death is so powerful that no one can defeat it.

Not doctors or lawyers or priests or kings or even mothers!

121

But God sent an unexpected hero.

People thought that God's chosen King would show up on a horse, with a sword in His hand, and sit on a throne. They thought He would defeat death by using His muscles and weapons.

But He didn't. God's chosen King showed up on a donkey, got nails put in His hands, and then was hung on a cross.

God's chosen King faced death,
and it looked like He lost,
but He didn't.

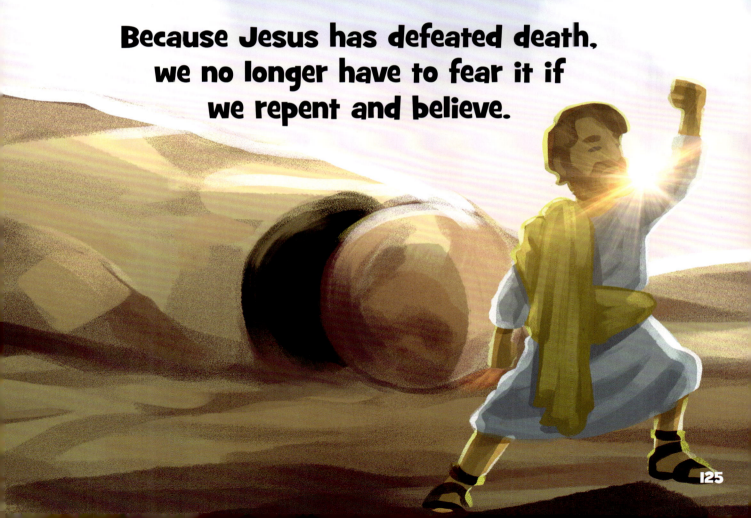

Now we come to the incredible victory.

Jesus didn't stay dead. He couldn't.
Death could not hold Him. Jesus came
back to life again, SMASHING death once
and for all, and He lives forever.

Because Jesus has defeated death,
we no longer have to fear it if
we repent and believe.

Just like David, the hero, became king
and sat on his throne,

Jesus, our Hero, is God's special chosen King,
and sits on heaven's throne forever.

"Where, O death, is your victory?

Where, O death, is your sting?"

The sting of death is sin,
and the power of sin is the law.

But thanks be to God!

He gives us the victory
through our Lord Jesus Christ.

I Corinthians 15:55-57 (NIV)

So next time you hear the wonderful true story about David and Goliath, remember... it's a story that tells us about Jesus!

This is a true story.

It comes from 2 Samuel Chapter 9 in your Bible.

This story has some hidden things to look out for.

See if you can find them:

Israel had a great king called David. (You might remember him, he killed the evil giant Goliath.)

There was also a poor orphaned beggar called Mephibosheth (meh-FIB-oh-sheth).

He hadn't always been poor. Once he had been part of another king's family. A king called Saul.

King Saul hated David because God had chosen David to be the next king, and on many occasions Saul had tried killing him.

Saul had made himself David's enemy.

Saul had a son called Jonathan.

Jonathan was David's best friend.

David and Jonathan cared about each other very much and promised to always take care of each other, and each others families.

One day, King Saul died in battle, and sadly, so did his son Jonathan.

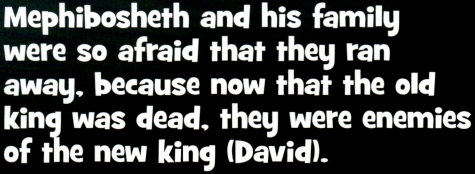

Mephibosheth and his family were so afraid that they ran away, because now that the old king was dead, they were enemies of the new king (David).

As they ran, Mephibosheth's nurse fell and dropped him, breaking both of his legs. He was never able to walk again after that accident.

Years passed, and one day King David asked if there was anyone left in Saul's family. Everyone thought he would want to put them in prison or even kill them.

After all, they were enemies, and that's what usually happened to the king's enemies.

Mephibosheth, now an orphan, was the only one left alive from Saul's family. To make matters worse, he was crippled in both of his legs so he couldn't even run away and hide.

He must have been so afraid, and thought the worst was coming.

But David was kind and gracious.

Instead of putting Mephibosheth in prison or even killing him, King David adopted him as his own son.

He gave him a place to live and took care of all of his needs.

He even left a place at the king's table for him to eat with the king and his family any time he wished. This orphan had a new home and a new family.

But why would he do that? Mephibosheth didn't deserve that level of kindness.

"For Jonathan's sake," said David. "My dear friend who died."

King David gave him good things because someone else deserved them, his dear friend Jonathan.

So Mephibosheth wasn't a poor orphan anymore. The king had accepted him, adopted him, and given him a home and a new family.

All for the sake of Jonathan.

142

Did you find the hidden pictures?

They can help to summarize our story.

A great king

An enemy of the king

The king's dear friend who died

A new family

What do you think?

Is this a story that tells us to adopt people in wheelchairs?
NO.

Is this a story that teaches us that our enemies will die in battle?
NO.

So, what's this story really about?

This story is about
JESUS!

But how?

The Bible says that God is the greatest king of all.

It also tells us that we have made ourselves God's enemies by doing, saying, and thinking things that God warns us not to.

(The Bible calls that sin.)

The Bible says that we will stand before God's throne one day. We can't run away from that or hide either.

But instead of punishment, God offers us peace and even offers to adopt us as His own sons and daughters.

God offers us a home and a future and for us to always be with Him.

"But why would God do such a wonderful thing?" you might ask.

Because we deserve it?

No.

Because God looks at Jesus, who died, and says,

"For His sake."

Jesus was perfect and good all the time. He never did anything wrong, or ever disobeyed God's rules.

Jesus was the perfect son, the perfect friend.

Jesus died for our sins. And God remembered Jesus' death and rewards us because of Jesus' goodness.

149

Mephibosheth was given the choice to stay as an enemy of the king, or become his son.

God gives us that choice as well.

Mephibosheth chose wisely.
What will you choose?

But you are a chosen people, a royal priesthood, a holy nation, God's special possession, that you may declare the praises of him who called you out of darkness into his wonderful light.

1 Peter 2:9 (NIV)

So next time you hear the wonderful, true story about David and Mephibosheth, remember... it's a story that tells us about Jesus!

True Stories from the New Testament

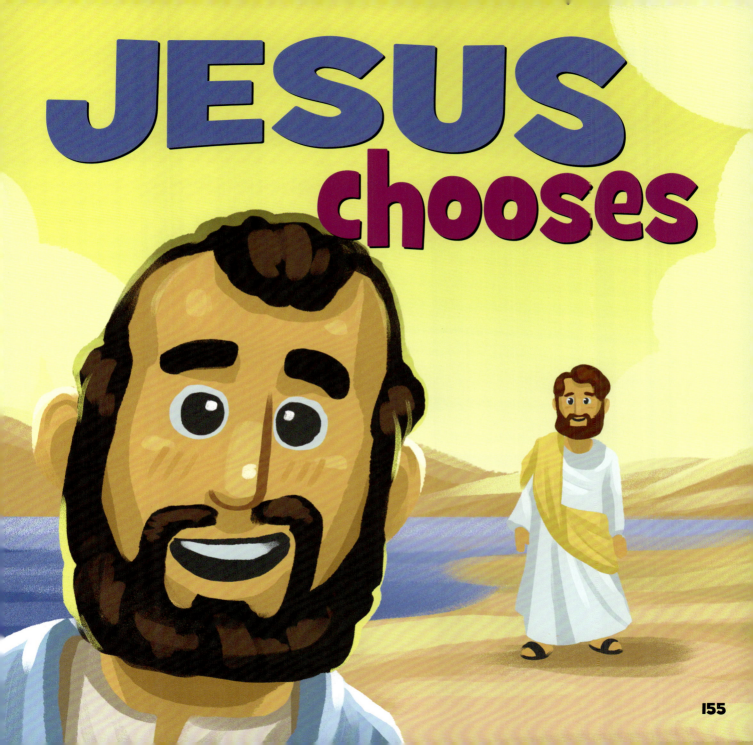

JESUS chooses

This is a true story about Jesus.

It comes from Luke Chapter 5
in your Bible.

Simon was a fisherman. He worked on his boat with his little brother, Andrew.

Simon loved to fish, but probably wondered if there was more to life.

One day Jesus was standing beside a lake. He was teaching a group of people, but it was too crowded. Jesus looked and saw a man called Simon working in his boat on the shore.

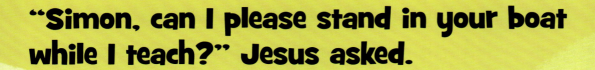

"Simon, can I please stand in your boat while I teach?" Jesus asked.

"Sure," said Simon.

Simon was a little grumpy because he had worked hard, fishing all night, but had caught nothing.

As Jesus finished teaching the crowd from Simon's boat, Simon listened to what Jesus said.

He had never heard anyone teach the way Jesus did.

When He had finished speaking, He said to Simon, "Push out into the deep water. Let down your nets and let's go fishing."

Simon said to Him, "Teacher, we already fished all night, and we caught nothing. But if you say so, I will let down the nets."

There was something special about Jesus, Simon could tell, but he didn't know what.

Simon and Jesus took the boat out to the deep water. Simon threw the net overboard, and as soon as he had, they caught so many fish, the net started to break. They called to their friends working in the other boat to come and help them.

They came, and both boats were so full of fish they began to sink!

Simon was shocked. He had never seen this many fish before in his whole life!

He was amazed, alarmed, and surprised.

There was something VERY special about Jesus! Something wonderful and special and great.

But then Simon realized something.

Someone as special and important as Jesus shouldn't have anything to do with him. Simon was a very unimportant, ordinary person. Simon thought it wasn't right for Jesus to spend time with him.

Simon sighed and bowed his face low, and said, "Go away from me, Lord, because I am a sinful man. I don't deserve to be around you."

Jesus looked at Simon and smiled.

Simon didn't realize it yet, but Jesus wasn't on this boat by accident. He had chosen Simon's boat on purpose.

He had chosen Simon to be His friend.

"Do not be afraid, Simon," Jesus said.

"Come follow me."

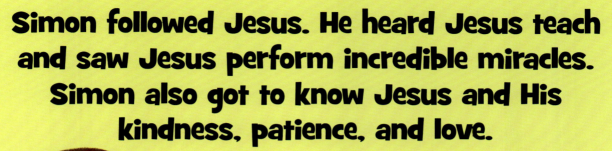

Simon followed Jesus. He heard Jesus teach and saw Jesus perform incredible miracles. Simon also got to know Jesus and His kindness, patience, and love.

Simon even saw Jesus do things he didn't understand.

Simon was there when Jesus was arrested, and then put on a cross to die.

Simon didn't understand how they could do that.

Then three days later, Jesus came back from the dead, defeating death once and for all.

Simon started to understand.

There was more to life than just fishing after all.

You might know Simon by the nickname that Jesus gave him; Peter.

Peter spent the rest of his life telling people the wonderful news that God had sent His Son Jesus to rescue them from sin and death. Even though Peter let Jesus down sometimes, Jesus never let him down, ever.

Jesus chose Simon.

Jesus has chosen you to be His friend. You might not be the strongest, the smartest, or even the tallest. You might not think you are very special at all, but Jesus loves you anyway.

But now, this is what the LORD says — he who created you, Jacob, he who formed you, Israel: "Do not fear, for I have redeemed you; I have summoned you by your name; you are mine."

Isaiah 43:1 (NIV)

There is no one else like Jesus.

You can read this story in the Bible. It was written by a man called Luke.

Luke was a researcher who diligently interviewed people who knew Jesus and saw the things He did. He compiled these true stories into a book in the Bible called the Gospel of Luke.

Luke tells us how amazing Jesus is and how He can change people's lives.

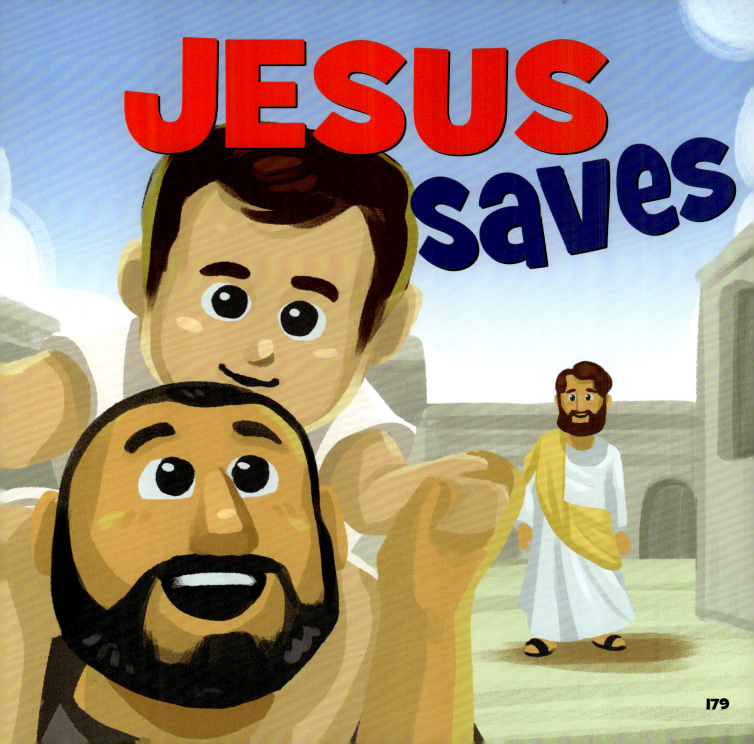

JESUS saves

This is a true story about Jesus.

**It comes from John
Chapter 4 in your Bible.**

In a town called Capernaum, there lived a man who worked for King Herod. He was an important man, and when he gave orders, people listened and obeyed.

The man's son was very sick. He had ordered the doctors to help, and even though they tried, there was nothing they could do. The little boy grew sicker and sicker, and they knew that soon he would die.

The man knew that there were things like sickness and death that no ordinary person could control, not even a person as important as himself.

One morning, the man heard that Jesus was in a nearby town. He had heard about Jesus before. The man knew that Jesus was no ordinary person and that He could do things no one had ever done before.

He knew that Jesus told people to believe that He was God's special chosen king, but since the man had never seen Jesus do any miracles himself, he wasn't sure what to believe.

The man hurried to see Jesus. He thought if he could get Jesus to come back with him, then maybe his little boy could get better.

The man spent all morning running, and got to the town just after lunchtime.

"Please!" the man begged. "Please come to my house and heal my son. He is dying."

Jesus turned and looked at the man and said something strange.

"Some people don't believe unless they see with their own eyes."

Jesus was talking about him.

"Please, come with me" he said.

Jesus shook his head and smiled.

"Go home," He said.
"Your son will live."

Perhaps some people in the crowd didn't understand what Jesus was saying. Maybe some of them thought Jesus was refusing to help, but the man understood.

Jesus wanted the man to trust Him, even if he didn't get to see it with his own eyes.

The man trusted in what Jesus said, and his heart filled with hope. He believed that Jesus was able to do this and that his son would be okay.

The next morning, the man began his walk home, and while he was still on his way, some of his servants met him on the road.

"You won't believe what happened!" they laughed and cheered.

"Your son is healed. Yesterday, all of a sudden, he just got better." The man smiled, and tears came to his eyes.

"What time did he get better?" he asked.

"Right after lunchtime," his servants responded.

Exactly the time that Jesus had said so.

The man went home and saw his son.

He was completely healed!

He told his family what Jesus had done for them, and they all trusted and believed that Jesus was God's special chosen King.

Jesus healed the man's son with only a word.

He didn't even need to come to the man's house. No one else has power like that.

Jesus gave the man the choice to trust Him, and the man was not disappointed or let down.

Jesus never lets us down
when we trust Him.

I love the LORD, for he heard my voice;
he heard my cry for mercy.

Because he turned his ear to me,
I will call on him as long as I live.

Psalm 116:1–2 (NIV)

There is no one else like Jesus.

You can read this story in the Bible. It was written by a man called John, one of Jesus disciples (followers).

John wrote plenty of other amazing and wonderful things that Jesus said and did. You can find the rest of John's true stories about Jesus in the Bible in the Gospel of John.

This is a true story about Jesus.

It comes from Matthew Chapter 8 in your Bible.

One day Jesus was walking with His disciples when a man with leprosy met him on the road.

(Leprosy is a terrible skin disease.)

The man was lonely, he was sick, and he was afraid. The people around him called him unclean.

The man's doctors couldn't help him, and no one the man knew was willing to be near him anymore. They would all run away when they saw him coming, or throw rocks at him until he went away. They were afraid they would get leprosy too.

He couldn't even go to the temple to give God a gift or to pray, because lepers weren't allowed there.

Jesus didn't run away,
and He didn't tell him to
go away, either.

Jesus didn't even frown when He smelled the man's dirty clothes and sick skin.

"Lord, if you are willing, you can make me clean," the man said.

He believed that Jesus was able to make him better, but he wasn't sure if Jesus would be willing.

Jesus smiled. Then He did something that no one had done for a very long time.

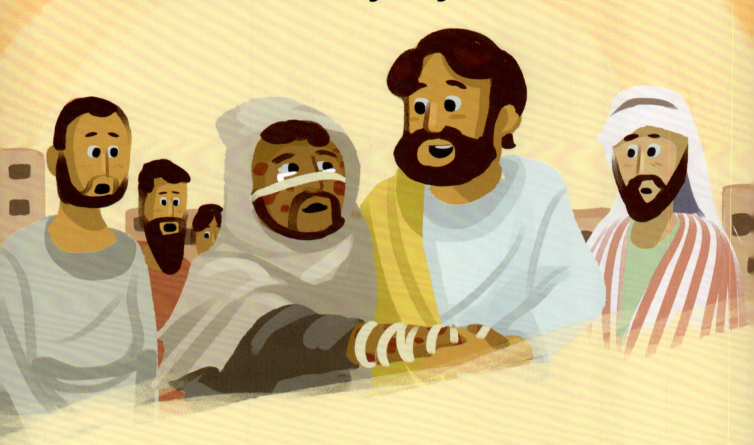

He reached out His hand and touched the man.

The man had missed being touched, being hugged, and being loved. He missed his wife and his friends, he missed going to the temple, and he missed his home. His body was sore and it hurt all over. He was tired, lonely, and sad.

For so long the man had been too sick to be loved. No one had wanted to be near him.

But not Jesus.

"I am willing," Jesus said, still smiling. "Be clean."

Suddenly the man felt different. He looked at his hands and arms. They looked different. He couldn't feel the pain of his sores anymore. His sores and spots were gone!

The man laughed in excitement and looked down at his feet and legs. He felt his face and his ears. They felt normal again!

The leprosy was gone!

"Go to the temple and give God a gift," said Jesus.

"You are most welcome there."

218

The man went to the temple to thank God for what Jesus had done for him.

219

Then he returned home to see his family and friends.

He had missed them so much, and thanks to Jesus, he could be with them again.

Jesus loved and accepted the man even before he was cured.

No one else would do that.

He healed the man, and He even gave the man the ability to give a gift to God.

No one else could do that.

Jesus was able,
and He was willing.

Jesus is always
willing to help us when
we call out to Him.

There is no one else like JESUS.

Heal me, Lord, and I will be healed;
save me and I will be saved, for you
are the one I praise.

Jeremiah 17:14 (NIV)

You can read this true story in the Bible. This story was written down by a man called Matthew, one of Jesus' disciples (followers).

Matthew saw and heard many things that Jesus did and said. He wrote them down for us so we could learn about how wonderful Jesus is.

You can find his stories about Jesus in the Bible in the Gospel of Matthew.

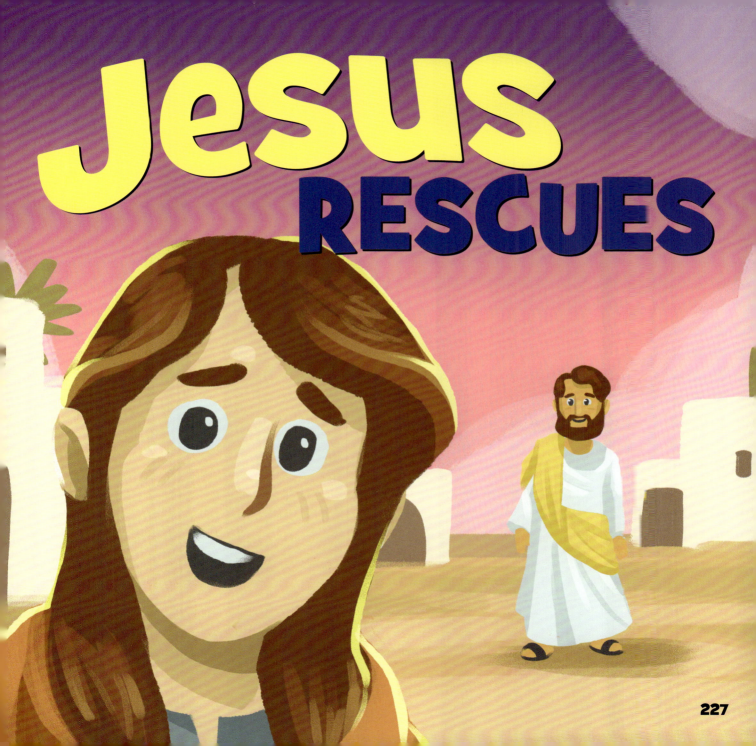

JESUS RESCUES

This is a true story about Jesus.

It comes from John
Chapter 8 in your Bible.

Jesus was in the temple teaching the people about God.

While He was speaking, some Pharisees brought in a woman who had broken God's law. They put her in the middle of the crowd and demanded Jesus listen as they explained the horrible thing that she had done.

"This deserves a huge punishment!" they said.

"What do you think?" they said to Jesus.

The teachers of the law were trying to get Jesus to make a mistake.

They knew He was kind, and that He taught that God was willing to forgive people. They thought He would tell them what she had done didn't matter. Then they could tell everyone that Jesus didn't care about God's laws.

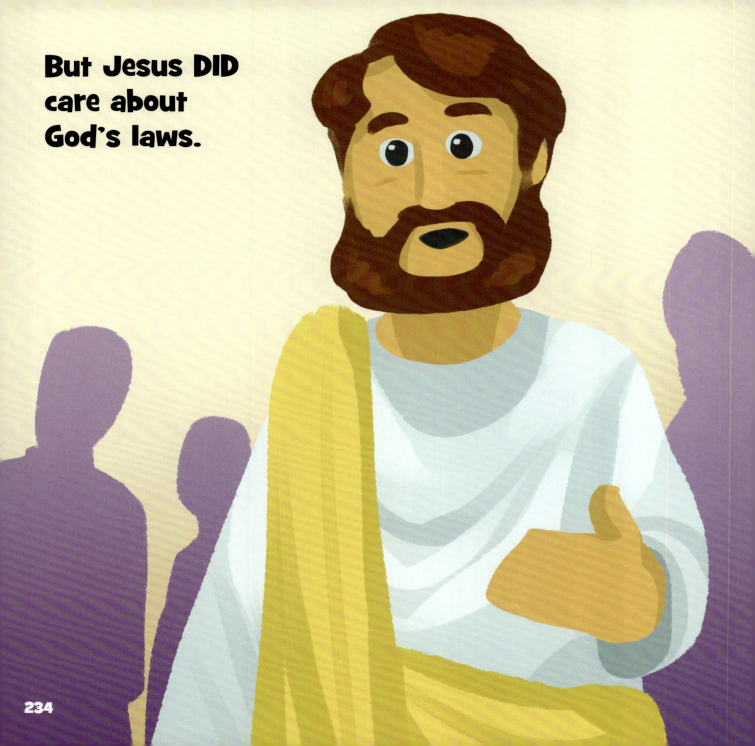

But Jesus DID care about God's laws.

Jesus looked at the woman.
She had broken God's law,
and she did deserve to
be punished.

But Jesus loved her, even though she was guilty.

The teachers of the law grew impatient, and they asked Him again.

"What do you think should be done?" they said.

Jesus turned to them and said:

"All right, but let the one who has never broken God's law be the one to punish her."

The Pharisees became silent. They each knew that they had also broken God's law. As good as they thought they were, deep down they knew that they weren't perfect.

There was only one person there who had never broken God's laws.

Jesus.

The Pharisees felt guilty. One by one, they walked away, until there was only Jesus left with the woman.

Then Jesus said to her, "Where did they go? Is there anyone left who wants to see you punished?"

"No, Lord," she said.

Jesus smiled at her. "Neither do I. Go and live the way God wants you to."

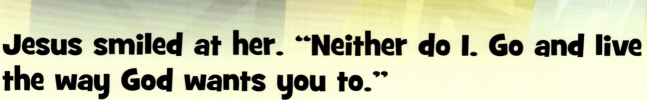

Jesus rescued the woman from those who wanted her to be punished, even though she deserved it. Jesus loved her and stepped in to rescue her when no one else would.

Jesus knew that anyone who breaks God's law must be punished, so He took that punishment Himself.

A short while after this story,
Jesus died on a cross.

Not just for this woman, but to rescue everyone who has ever broken God's laws.

Even people like the Pharisees.

Jesus came back from the dead, proving that He had paid for our sin, and because of this, we can trust Him to rescue us!

For God did not send his Son into the world to condemn the world, but to save the world through him.

John 3:17 (NIV)

There is no one else like Jesus.

You can read this story in the Bible. It was written by a man called John, one of Jesus disciples (followers).

John wrote plenty of other amazing and wonderful things that Jesus said and did. You can find the rest of John's true stories about Jesus in the Bible in the Gospel of John.

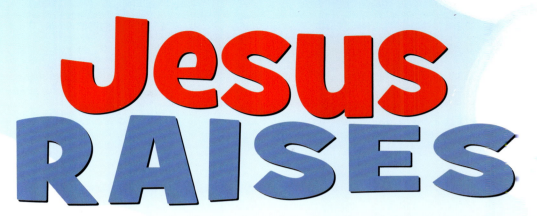

This is a true story about Jesus.

It comes from John Chapter 11
in your Bible.

Jesus had a friend named Lazarus.

Jesus often visited Lazarus and his sisters when He was in town.

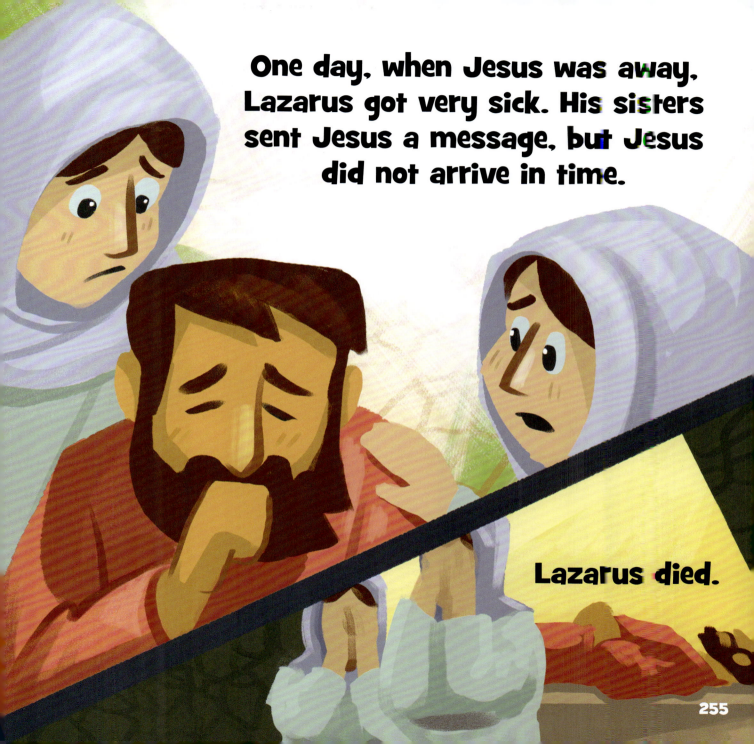

One day, when Jesus was away, Lazarus got very sick. His sisters sent Jesus a message, but Jesus did not arrive in time.

Lazarus died.

255

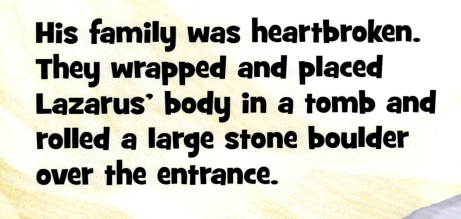

His family was heartbroken. They wrapped and placed Lazarus' body in a tomb and rolled a large stone boulder over the entrance.

Four days later, Jesus arrived.

"If only you had been here," said Lazarus' sisters. "Our brother would not have died."

They both believed that Jesus could have healed Lazarus, but that only God Himself could raise the dead.

257

"I am the One who raises the dead," said Jesus.

Jesus saw how heartbroken they were, and all the damage that death had done.

Jesus wept.

He was heartbroken too.

Jesus went to the tomb.
"Take away the stone," He said.

They took away the stone.

Jesus prayed.

Then He called, "Lazarus, come out!"

264

**The tomb was silent,
and then there came a noise.**

It was Lazarus.

He was alive! He came out of the tomb, still wrapped in his grave clothes.

Everyone was amazed.
They had never seen
anything like this before!

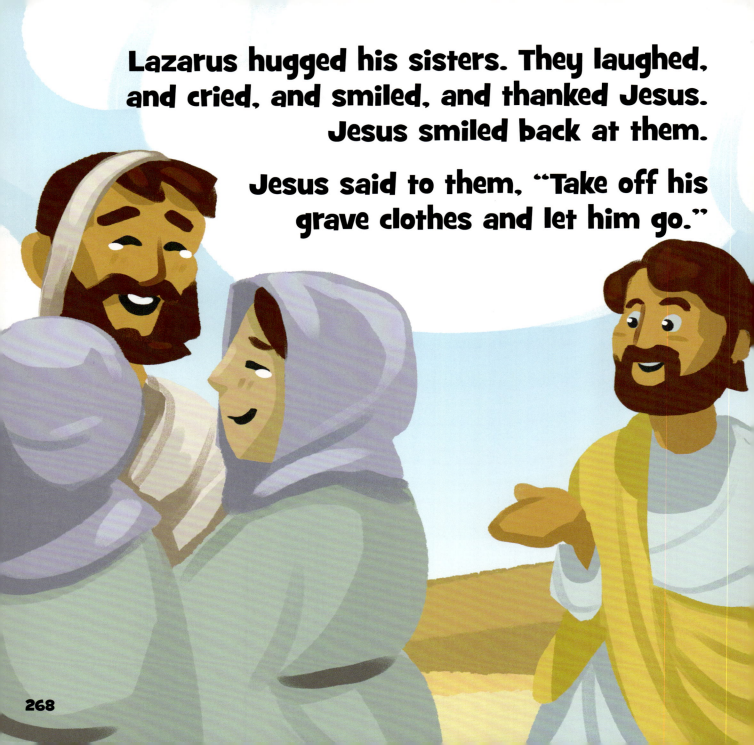

Lazarus hugged his sisters. They laughed, and cried, and smiled, and thanked Jesus. Jesus smiled back at them.

Jesus said to them, "Take off his grave clothes and let him go."

268

Jesus was with Lazarus'
sisters in their heartbreak.
He even shared it with them.

He is with us when bad
things happen as well.

Then Jesus raised Lazarus from the dead.
No one else could do that.

Jesus was able.

Jesus is more powerful than death.

There is no one else like Jesus.

Jesus said to her, "I am the resurrection and the life. The one who believes in me will live, even though they die; and whoever lives by believing in me will never die. Do you believe this?"

John 11:25-26 (NIV)

You can read this true story in the Bible. It was written by a man called John, one of Jesus' disciples (followers).

John was with Jesus when Jesus raised Lazarus, and he wrote down what he saw, and heard, and experienced.

John wrote plenty of other amazing and wonderful things that Jesus said and did. You can find the rest of John's stories about Jesus in the Bible in the Gospel of John.

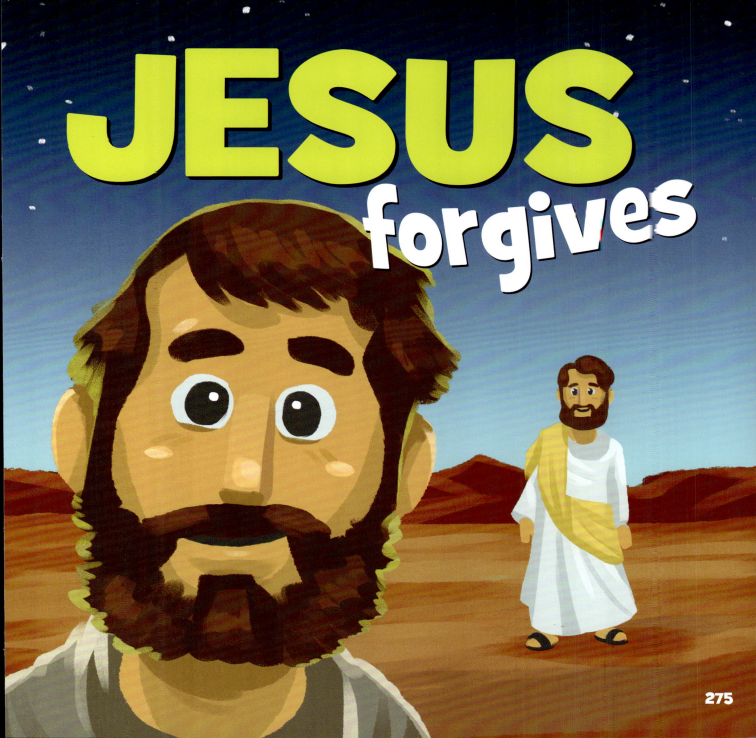

JESUS forgives

This is a true story about Jesus.

It comes from Luke Chapter 23 in your Bible.

On a hill outside of Jerusalem, Jesus hung dying on a wooden cross. People around Him mocked Him, others booed, and others cheered. Jesus' friends stood confused and crying, unsure what to do. Next to Him were two other crosses, on which two criminals hung, a rebel and the robber.

Both the rebel and the robber
had broken the law
and were being punished.

Jesus had not broken any laws.
He had only done good,
all of the time.

He didn't deserve to be punished.

"Hey, you!" the rebel yelled.

"I heard you say you are God's son. If you are, then why don't you come down and save yourself and us too!"

The thief hung there too, silently watching. He had also mocked Jesus as they had walked up the hill. But Jesus hadn't yelled back, or cursed, or even frowned at them. Jesus didn't call the soldiers names or threaten them. He didn't even complain that this wasn't fair.

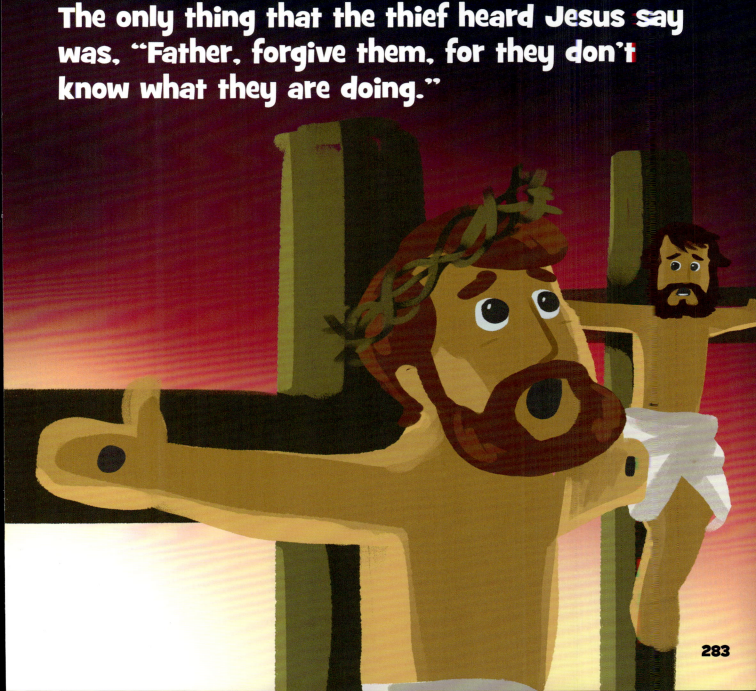

The only thing that the thief heard Jesus say was, "Father, forgive them, for they don't know what they are doing."

283

The thief knew that
he was guilty and
deserved to be there.

He also knew that Jesus wasn't guilty of any crime. He had never seen anyone react the way Jesus did. He had never seen anyone love people and pray for them, like Jesus did, even for the Romans who had nailed Him there.

The rebel started to mock Jesus again. But this time the thief spoke up.

"Have you no fear of God? You're getting the same punishment as Jesus. We deserve this because we did the wrong thing, but not him — he did nothing to deserve this."

The thief looked at Jesus.

He must have known Jesus was special, and this wouldn't be the end for Him. He believed Jesus was God's special chosen King.

He didn't deserve to ask for help. He wasn't a good man, and he knew it. "Please, Jesus," the thief asked. "Please remember me when you come into Your kingdom."

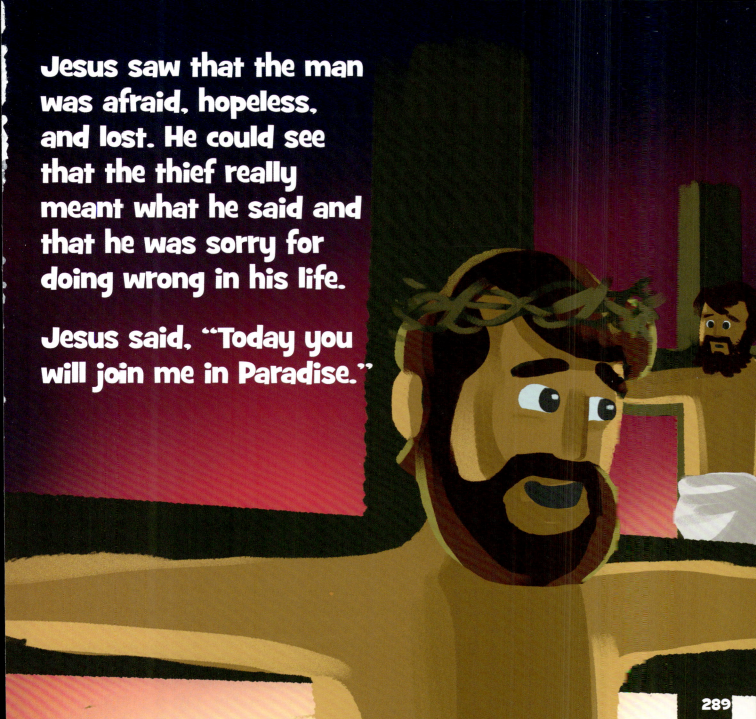

Jesus saw that the man was afraid, hopeless, and lost. He could see that the thief really meant what he said and that he was sorry for doing wrong in his life.

Jesus said, "Today you will join me in Paradise."

289

Paradise...

The thief was speechless. Even in the middle of His own suffering, Jesus had given the thief hope when there was hopelessness, and a promise of new life in place of despair.

Later that day, Jesus breathed His last breath and died. Some time afterward, so did the rebel and the robber.

Both the rebel and the robber were guilty and deserving of the punishments they got.

The thief, thanks to Jesus,
met Jesus again in Paradise.

Jesus forgave the thief for his crimes. He forgave him and gave him a place in Paradise.

It wasn't because the thief had done good deeds. It was only because he believed in Jesus' forgiveness and promise.

No one can open the doors to heaven except for Jesus.

Jesus loved the thief and accepted him with open arms.

Jesus loves you too. He has paid the price of your sins by dying on the Cross, and heaven is open only because of Him.

Jesus is ready to forgive you as well. All you have to do is to ask forgiveness for your sins and believe in Him to save you.

The Lord our God is merciful and forgiving, even though we have rebelled against him.

Daniel 9:9 (NIV)

There is no one else like Jesus.

You can read this story in the Bible. It was written by a man called Luke.

Luke was a researcher who diligently interviewed people who knew Jesus and saw the things He did. He compiled these true stories into a book in the Bible called the Gospel of Luke.

Luke tells us how amazing Jesus is and how He can change people's lives.

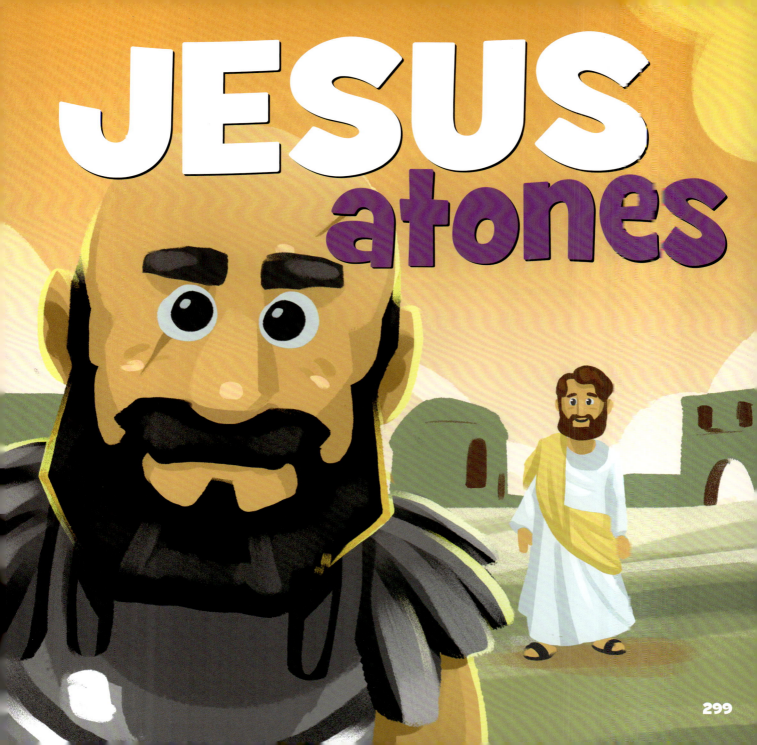

JESUS
atones

This is a true story about Jesus.

It comes from Luke Chapter 23 in your Bible.

Barabbas (buh-RAB-us) was a rebel, a criminal, and even a murderer.

He had tried to run, but had been caught and was now sitting in prison. The Romans had prepared a cross for him. Barabbas knew he would have to carry that cross out of the city, and be nailed and hung on it until he died. That was his punishment.

Deep down, Barabbas
must have known
he deserved it.

Barabbas sat in chains. He could hear a lot of noise outside of people yelling and cheering.

Pontius Pilate, the governor, called for everyone to be quiet.

Barabbas listened carefully to what Pilate had to say.

"You told me this man was guilty of trying to start a rebellion. But I have spoken to Him and looked at the evidence and I don't believe He's guilty of anything, so I am going to release Him."

Perhaps Barabbas wondered who Pilate was talking about. It definitely wasn't him.

The crowd became angry and started yelling loudly. This time Barabbas heard his name. "Release Barabbas to us and arrest this man instead!" they chanted.

Barabbas had to be surprised by this. "But this man is innocent!" Pilate said back to the crowd.

The crowd shouted even louder,
"Crucify Him! Crucify Him!!"

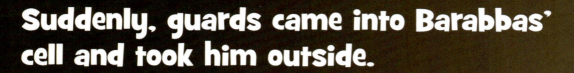

Suddenly, guards came into Barabbas' cell and took him outside.

Barabbas stood in front of the crowd and looked at Pilate.

Then he saw the man everyone was talking about.

It was Jesus.

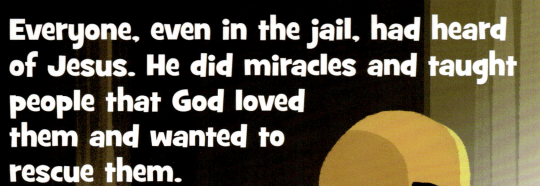

Everyone, even in the jail, had heard of Jesus. He did miracles and taught people that God loved them and wanted to rescue them.

Barabbas probably knew that Jesus wasn't a bad man at all.

Pilate was right.

Jesus was innocent.

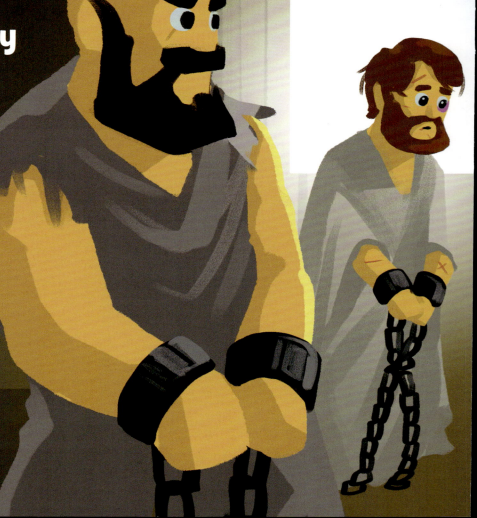

Jesus was also standing tied up. "The soldiers must have done that to Him," Barabbas possibly thought.

He was beaten, bruised, and badly bleeding.

Pilate called to the crowd, "What evil has this man done? He is innocent!"

The crowd cheered, booed, and yelled. They screamed and shouted, and in the end, Pilate agreed. The guards came over to Barabbas and undid his chains.

Barabbas was free to go.

Jesus looked up at Barabbas with love in His eyes. Barabbas had never seen anyone look at him that way before.

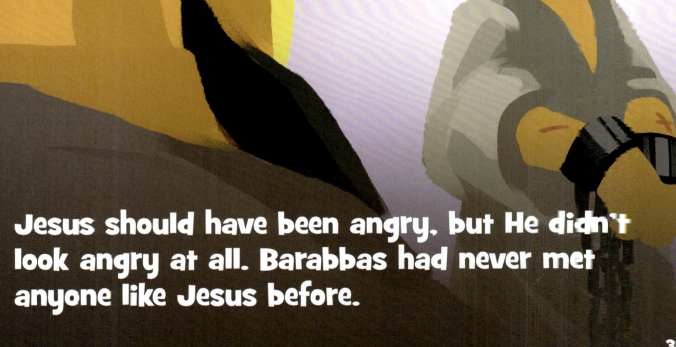

Jesus should have been angry, but He didn't look angry at all. Barabbas had never met anyone like Jesus before.

Soon the guards took Jesus over
to the cross and forced Him to carry it.

Barabbas was free,
and Jesus, the innocent one,
was now carrying his cross.

That day Jesus, the innocent man, died.

And the guilty man, Barabbas, was freed and given a chance to start a new life.

The Bible says that each of us has broken God's laws, and that makes us guilty and deserving of punishment.

But Jesus came to Earth, and even though He was innocent, He paid for our sins and guilt by dying on the cross.

Just like Jesus took Barabbas' place, the Bible says He has taken our place too. When Jesus died on the Cross, He was paying for all our sins.

No one else could do that.

Jesus gave Barabbas the chance of a new life. Jesus does the same for us as well. He defeated death and is still alive.

For Christ also suffered once for sins, the righteous for the unrighteous, to bring you to God. He was put to death in the body but made alive in the Spirit.

1 Peter 3:18 (NIV)

There is no one else like Jesus.

You can read this story in the Bible. It was written by a man called Luke.

Luke was a researcher who diligently interviewed people who knew Jesus and saw the things He did. He compiled these true stories into a book in the Bible called the Gospel of Luke. Luke tells us how amazing Jesus is and how He can change people's lives.

Jesus COMFORTS

This is a true story about Jesus.

It comes from John Chapter 20 in your Bible.

Mary Magdalene (mag·duh·luhn) was a follower of Jesus. She had heard Him teach wonderful things about God. She had seen Him perform amazing miracles that no one else had ever done before.

She wasn't only his follower,
Mary was Jesus' friend.

Jesus was so powerful and wise and important, but He still had time for her. Whenever He spoke to her, He was always so kind. When He called her name, He said it as someone who really knew her and truly cared for her.

Mary thought that Jesus must be the Savior of the world. Three days ago, Jesus had been arrested.

Mary thought that everything would work out somehow, and that maybe Jesus would perform a miracle and get away.

The soldiers had taken Jesus to the temple where the priests had yelled at Him and called Him all sorts of horrible names. Then they had taken Him to the Roman governor, where Jesus had been beaten, and then sentenced to death.

She had then watched as the Roman soldiers nailed Jesus to a cross and hung Him up, and she cried in horror as Jesus breathed His last breath and then died.

Mary wondered what this meant. She knew Jesus was special, that He had power over nature and sickness. He had even raised other people from the dead, but now He was dead.

How could Jesus be the Savior of the world if He was dead?

Mary was confused, afraid, and heartbroken.

Early Sunday morning, Mary went to the tomb to visit where Jesus' body was placed. She wanted to make sure His body was buried properly, that He had nice smelling spices around Him. He was her friend and teacher, and she didn't know what else to do.

Mary wondered if the soldiers who stood guard over the tomb would push the large boulder aside for her.

When she arrived, the stone had already been moved aside and there were no soldiers anywhere.

Mary came to the front of the cave and saw two men dressed in white sitting where Jesus' body had been. Mary didn't notice, but they were angels.

What Mary did notice was that Jesus' body was gone. Mary burst into tears.

"Why are you crying?" they asked her.

"They have taken Jesus' body away, and I don't know where they have put it," she replied.

Mary went outside and saw a man she thought must be a gardener. Maybe he would know where Jesus' body was.

"Sir, if you have carried Him away, please tell me where you have put Him, and I will get Him," she said.

The man didn't tell her where the body was. He didn't say much. He just called her name, "Mary."

Mary paused.

How did the gardener know her name?
No one said her name like that.
No one except Jesus!

She turned toward Him and began to cry again. But this time, not in sadness or confusion or fear. Mary's heart was so happy and so full of joy!

Jesus was alive!

He IS the Savior of the world after all!

Jesus smiled at her. Mary wasn't afraid anymore. She wasn't confused. She wasn't heartbroken.

Mary ran home to tell Jesus' other disciples the good news!

Jesus loved His friends, and He loved everyone. He went to the Cross to pay for their sins so that they could have peace with God. He knew that there was no other way. No one else could pay for sin.

Jesus didn't stay dead. He is more powerful than death. More powerful than sin. More powerful than anything.

No one else could defeat death.

Jesus turned Mary's heartbreak, confusion, and fear into joy and hope. Because Jesus has paid for sin and defeated death, we can all have this same joy and hope. Joy because we can have peace with God, and hope because death is not the end for us.

We can all be comforted that we can go and be with God forever in heaven, thanks to Jesus.

Praise be to the God and Father of our Lord Jesus Christ, the Father of compassion and the God of all comfort...

2 Corinthians 1:3 (NIV)

There is no one else like Jesus.

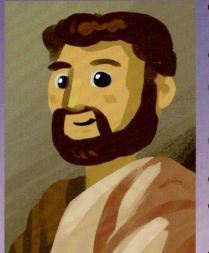

This story was written by a man called John, one of Jesus disciples (followers).

John wrote plenty of other amazing and wonderful things that Jesus said and did.

You can find the rest of John's stories about Jesus in the Bible in the Gospel of John.

Words to Know!

Throughout this book, you may remember some of the following words. Use these definitions to help you better understand what they mean. The next time you read this book, watch for the following words in the sentences.

Adopted: When a child becomes part of a new family, just like how God lovingly adopts us into His family when we believe in Jesus.

Altar: A pile of rocks and wood where a sacrifice is placed and later burned.

Angel: God's special messengers who bring messages of love, protection, and guidance from Him.

Ashamed: Feeling bad or guilty about something you've done wrong.

Believe: Trusting in God and having faith in His love and promises.

Clean: Sometimes used in the Bible to mean healed and made whole.

Criminal: A person who breaks the law and does something wrong.

Crippled: When someone has difficulty moving or walking.

Crucify: When Jesus was nailed to the Cross and died for our sins.

Disciples: People who follow Jesus and learn from Him, choosing to live like Him and share His love with others.

Disobedient: Choosing not to follow God's loving rules.

Disobey: To choose to not follow directions or rules.

Forgiveness: Choosing to let go of anger and hurt when someone has done something wrong.

Grave: A place where people are buried after they die.

Guilty: Being responsible for doing something wrong or disobeying God's commands.

Heartbreak: Feeling very sad and hurt when something bad happens.

Hero: Someone who shows great courage and kindness, like Jesus, who saved us all.

Innocent: Doing nothing wrong and without guilt, like how Jesus was without sin and perfect.

Judgment: The punishment that happens when people decide to go against God's laws.

Leprosy: A terrible skin disease.

Merciful: Showing kindness and forgiveness, even when someone else doesn't deserve it.

Mercy: Showing kindness and forgiveness to someone who deserves punishment.

Miracles: Amazing things that only God can do, like healing the sick or calming storms.

Obey: Do what you are told to do.

Orphan: A child who doesn't have parents to take care of them.

Passover: A special holiday celebrated by Jewish people to remember when they were freed from slavery in Egypt.

Pharaoh: A powerful king who ruled Egypt long ago.

Pharisees: People who pretended to follow God's law but often added their own rules as well.

Promise: A commitment to do something.

Prophet: Someone who gives people messages from God.

Punishment: Something bad that happens when we get in trouble.

Rebellion: Choosing to go against God's loving rules and doing things our own way.

Redeemed: Being saved and set free from the power of sin through Jesus' sacrifice on the Cross.

Repent: Being truly sorry for our mistakes, asking God for forgiveness, and trying our best to do better.

Resurrection: To come back to life as Jesus did after dying on the Cross, showing us that there is hope for eternal life with God.

Sacrifice: The life of an animal given up to bring forgiveness to those who have sinned.

Saved: When God rescues us from our sins and gives us a new life.

Savior: Jesus, who came to rescue and save us from our sins, showing us God's love and giving us eternal life.

Sin: Doing something that you know is wrong based on God's Word, the Bible.

Sinful: Doing things that go against God's rules and hurt our relationship with Him.

Sorrow: A deep sadness often felt when something or someone is lost or hurt.

Suffering: Going through pain or bad times.

Summoned: When God calls us to do something special or important.

Surrender: To give up your freedom to someone else.

Temple: A special place where people worship and honor God.

Trust: Believing that someone will do what they say they will do.

Venomous: Something that can harm or poison us.

Victory: Winning or overcoming something difficult with God's help.

Wilderness: Often an empty desert place away from any cities.